LASAGNE

over 30 delicious pasta dishes

RECIPES AND PHOTOGRAPHY
BY SANDRA MAHUT

hardie grant books

CONTENTS

PRINCIPLES

Layers of filling, béchamel sauce and sheets of lasagne are alternated, topped with cheese and baked au gratin.

BÉCHAMEL SAUCE

This white sauce provides the smooth, creamy element of your lasagne. Homemade béchamel sauce should not be too thick, as you want the lasagne to be soft rather than heavy. It can be flavoured with any seasonings you like. Ready-made béchamel sauce works, too.

RECIPE FOR 600 ML (20½ FL OZ)

2 tablespoons butter
1 pinch of salt
4 tablespoons plain (all-purpose) flour
500 ml (17 fl oz) milk
1 pinch each of pepper and ground nutmeg

Melt the butter in a saucepan over a low heat. Sprinkle in the flour and salt, and whisk to form a paste. Add the milk, little by little, stirring constantly. The sauce should thicken and become smooth and creamy. Season with pepper and nutmeg.

TOMATO SAUCE

RECIPE FOR 500 ML (17 FL OZ)

3 tablespoons olive oil
1 garlic clove, crushed
500 g (1 lb 2 oz) passata (puréed tomatoes)
1 teaspoon each of sugar, salt and pepper

Gently heat the olive oil with the garlic in a saucepan. Add the passata and sugar, and simmer gently for 5–8 minutes. Season with salt and pepper.

RED OR WHITE?

Like a pizza, lasagne can be made with or without a tomato-based sauce. If you are not using a tomato-based sauce, just be sure that your filling is liquid enough to cook the pasta.

LASAGNE SHEETS

Dried lasagne: Generally pre-cooked, meaning you can use it without any preparation. Cover the sheets with a slightly liquid filling so that they become nice and soft.
Fresh lasagne: Tastier and thicker than dried lasagne.

CHEESE

Add in layers in addition to, or instead of, the béchamel sauce. Melted cheese adds richness and flavour.

COOKING AU GRATIN

Top with a layer of cheese for a crispy crust. Sprinkle with herbs to add flavour to the entire dish.

FLAVOURING

You can create whatever flavours you desire with the ingredients you have to hand (vegetables, herbs and spices). Use leftover roast chicken or make a stew from scratch for a lasagne for a special occasion.

HERBS
Fresh herbs such as basil, parsley, chives, coriander (cilantro) or chervil work well in lasagnes. Pick off the leaves and snip to flavour béchamel sauces or to finish atop grated cheese. Dried or frozen herbs can also be used as a substitute.

VEGETABLES
Added raw for quick recipes, roasted for a little more flavour, or boiled to make a soft purée.

SEASONINGS
Add bay leaves, thyme, rosemary, onions, garlic, etc. to flavour your fillings or béchamel sauces.

SPICES
The classic complement to béchamel sauce is traditionally nutmeg. But you can also use cumin, paprika or curry powder to spice up your fillings, giving more depth to the dish.

BOLOGNESE
lasagne

Serves 6
Preparation: 25 minutes
Cooking time: 30–40 minutes

2 teaspoons olive oil
1 onion, thinly sliced
1 garlic clove, chopped
500 g (1 lb 2 oz) minced
  (ground) beef
500 ml (17 fl oz) passata
  (puréed tomatoes)
1 tablespoon dried oregano
1 teaspoon herbes de Provence
salt and black pepper
12 sheets of dried or fresh lasagne
600 ml (20½ fl oz) béchamel
  sauce (see page 4)
200 g (7 oz/1½ cups)
  grated Emmental

40 × 20 cm (15¾ × 8 in) gratin dish

Preheat the oven to 180°C (350°F/Gas 4). Heat 1 teaspoon olive oil in a frying pan (skillet) and gently fry the onion and garlic until soft. Add the beef and stir well to break up any clumps. Incorporate the passata, oregano and herbes de Provence. Season with salt and pepper.

Grease the gratin dish with the remaining 1 teaspoon olive oil. Lay 3 sheets of lasagne in the bottom of the dish, side by side, then alternate layers of meat and tomato sauce, lasagne and béchamel sauce. Repeat the process, finishing with a layer of béchamel sauce. Top with grated cheese and bake in the oven for 30–40 minutes.

MEAT

ROAST CHICKEN
lasagne

Serves 6
Preparation: 20 minutes
Cooking time: 30 minutes

400 g (14 oz) roast chicken
1 red (bell) pepper
½ green (bell) pepper
dash of olive oil
1 garlic clove, thinly sliced
1 red onion, thinly sliced
400 g (14 oz) passata
  (puréed tomatoes)
1 tablespoon tomato purée (paste)
salt
3 sprigs of fresh thyme or
  3 teaspoons of dried thyme
600 ml (20½ fl oz) béchamel
  sauce (see page 4)
12 sheets of dried or fresh lasagne
80 g (2¾ oz/½ cup) grated Comté
small bunch of chives, chopped

40 × 20 cm (15¾ × 8 in) gratin dish

Preheat the oven to 180°C (350°F/Gas 4). Tear the roast chicken into thin pieces, discarding the skin and bones. Cut the peppers in half, remove the seeds and slice finely.

Heat the olive oil in a frying pan (skillet) and sauté the garlic, onion and peppers for 5 minutes. Add the passata and tomato purée, and stir well. Simmer for a few minutes with the lid on. Season with salt.

Stir the thyme into the béchamel sauce.

Pour a little béchamel sauce into the bottom of the gratin dish. Lay 3 sheets of lasagne in the bottom of the dish, side by side, then alternate layers of pepper sauce, lasagne, roast chicken and béchamel sauce. Repeat the process, finishing with béchamel sauce. Top with grated Comté and sprinkle with chopped chives. Bake in the oven for 30–35 minutes.

MEAT

CHICKEN AND BACON
lasagne

Serves 6
Preparation: 35 minutes
Cooking time: 40 minutes

500 g (1 lb 2 oz) chicken
   breast, roughly chopped
1 garlic clove
1 shallot, chopped
200 g (7 oz) smoked bacon
   slices, chopped
2 tablespoons olive oil
500 ml (17 fl oz) tomato sauce
   (see page 4)
300 g (10½ oz) button
   mushrooms, quartered
small bunch of parsley, chopped
salt and black pepper
12 sheets of dried or fresh lasagne
250 g (9 oz/1⅔ cup) grated
   smoked cheese or mozzarella

CHICKEN BÉCHAMEL SAUCE*
50 g (1¾ oz/¼ cup) butter
50 g (1¾ oz/⅓ cup) plain
   (all-purpose) flour
1 pinch of salt
500 ml (17 fl oz) chicken stock

*or 600 ml (20½ fl oz) béchamel
   sauce (see page 4)

40 × 20 cm (15¾ × 8 in) gratin dish

Preheat the oven to 180°C (350°F/Gas 4). In a food processor, blitz the chicken, garlic, shallot and bacon. Heat 1 tablespoon olive oil in a frying pan (skillet), then add the chicken mixture, using a wooden spoon to break up any clumps. Cook for a few minutes, then stir in the tomato sauce. Simmer for 10–15 minutes.

For the chicken béchamel sauce, melt the butter in a saucepan over a low heat. Sprinkle with flour and salt, then whisk constantly to form a paste. Pour in the stock, little by little, stirring continuously, and cook for a few minutes. The sauce should thicken and become smooth and creamy.

Heat the remaining 1 tablespoon olive oil in a frying pan. Sauté the mushrooms for 3 minutes, until browned. Add the chopped parsley and season with salt and pepper.

Pour a little béchamel sauce into the bottom of the gratin dish. Lay 3 sheets of lasagne in the bottom of the dish, side by side, then alternate layers of chicken sauce, lasagne, béchamel sauce, cheese and mushrooms. Repeat the process, finishing with a layer of béchamel sauce and topping with cheese. Bake in the oven for 40 minutes.

MEAT

PUMPKIN AND SAUSAGE
lasagne

Serves 6
Preparation: 50 minutes
Cooking time: 30–40 minutes

500 g (1 lb 2 oz) pumpkin (squash)
50 ml (1¾ fl oz) olive oil
flaked sea salt
3 sprigs of rosemary
100 g (3½ oz) cooked
  white chicken meat
500 g (1 lb 2 oz) sausage meat
1 garlic clove
200 ml (7 fl oz) chicken stock
600 ml (20½ fl oz) béchamel
  sauce (see page 4)
12 sheets of dried or fresh lasagne
200 g (7 oz/1⅓ cup)
  grated Emmental

40 × 20 cm (15¾ × 8 in) gratin dish

Preheat the oven to 180°C (350°F/Gas 4). Peel and slice the pumpkin and lay the slices on a baking tray lined with greaseproof paper. Drizzle with most of the olive oil, then sprinkle with a pinch of salt and the leaves of 1 rosemary sprig. Roast in the oven for 30 minutes. This stage can be performed the day before making the lasagne.

In a food processor, blitz the chicken, sausage meat, garlic and leaves of 1 sprig of rosemary. Heat the remaining olive oil in a frying pan (skillet), add the meat mixture and brown over a medium heat. Pour in the chicken stock, stir and simmer for 5 minutes.

Pick the leaves of the remaining sprig of rosemary, chop finely and add to the béchamel sauce.

Preheat the oven to 180°C (350°F/Gas 4). Pour 1 teaspoon olive oil and a little béchamel sauce into the bottom of the gratin dish. Lay 3 sheets of lasagne in the bottom of the dish, side by side, then alternate layers of chopped meat, lasagne, roast pumpkin and béchamel sauce. Repeat the process, finishing with pumpkin and a little béchamel sauce. Sprinkle with cheese. Bake in the oven for 30–40 minutes.

MEAT

12

TURKEY AND TOMATO
lasagne

Serves 6
Preparation: 25 minutes
Cooking time: 35 minutes

500 g (1 lb 2 oz) turkey breasts
2 garlic cloves
150 g (5½ oz) pancetta
2 teaspoons olive oil
1 shallot, thinly sliced
300 ml (10 fl oz) chicken stock
1 teaspoon herbes de Provence
400 ml (13½ fl oz) tomato
   sauce (preferably homemade
   tomato sauce using cherry
   tomatoes, see page 4)
12 sheets of dried or fresh lasagne
150 g (5½ oz) taleggio, sliced
salt
fresh thyme, to serve

40 × 20 cm (15¾ × 8 in) gratin dish

Preheat the oven to 180°C (350°F/Gas 4). In a food processor, blitz the turkey with 1 garlic clove and the pancetta. Heat 1 teaspoon olive oil in a frying pan (skillet) and fry the shallot for 5 minutes over a low heat. Add the turkey mixture and fry gently, until browned. Pour in the chicken stock and sprinkle in the herbes de Provence. Stir well and cook for about 5 minutes until the liquid has reduced.

Chop the remaining garlic clove and stir it into the tomato sauce.

Pour 1 teaspoon olive oil into the bottom of the gratin dish. Lay 3 sheets of lasagne in the bottom of the dish, side by side, then alternate layers of meat, lasagne and slices of taleggio. Repeat the process, finishing with the tomato sauce. Bake in the oven for 35 minutes. Sprinkle with thyme before serving.

MEAT

SAUSAGE AND RICOTTA
lasagne

Serves 6
Preparation: 20 minutes
Cooking time: 30 minutes

500 g (1 lb 2 oz) chipolatas
  or other pork sausages
2 tablespoons olive oil
60 g (2 oz) smoked
  bacon slices, diced
3 sage leaves, chopped
1 garlic clove, crushed
250 g (9 oz) cherry
  tomatoes, halved
150 ml (5 fl oz) tomato sauce
  (see page 4)
500 g (1 lb 2 oz/2 cups) ricotta
250 g (9 oz/1¼ cup) mascarpone
5 sprigs of basil, snipped
salt and black pepper
250 g (9 oz) mozzarella, sliced
12 sheets of dried or fresh lasagne
80 g (2¾ oz/¾ cup) grated
  Parmesan

40 × 20 cm (15¾ × 8 in) gratin dish

Preheat the oven to 180°C (350°F/Gas 4). Slice the sausage skin and remove the meat. Heat 1 tablespoon olive oil in a frying pan (skillet) and add the sausage meat, using a fork to break it up. Add the bacon, sage and garlic, and fry until the sausage meat is golden. Add the cherry tomatoes and the tomato sauce, then stir well. Cook for 5 minutes.

Mix together the ricotta, mascarpone, basil, 1 tablespoon olive oil and a pinch of salt. Add the mozzarella slices.

Pour 1 ladleful of the creamy cheese mixture into the bottom of the gratin dish. Lay 3 sheets of lasagne in the bottom of the dish, side by side, and then alternate layers of sausage and tomatoes, lasagne and creamy cheese. Repeat the process, finishing with creamy cheese. Season with pepper and sprinkle with Parmesan. Bake in the oven for 30 minutes.

MEAT

PORK AND PORCINI
lasagne

Serves 6
Preparation: 30 minutes
Cooking time: 30–40 minutes

450 g (1 lb) sweet potatoes
3 tablespoons olive oil
 + 1 teaspoon olive oil
2 tablespoons honey
1 teaspoon fleur de sel
 or flaked sea salt
freshly ground mixed peppercorns
600 g (1 lb 5 oz) pork neck
1 shallot
1 garlic clove
4 sprigs of parsley
1½ tablespoons oregano
300 g (10½ oz) fresh porcini
 mushrooms, chopped
200 ml (7 fl oz) single
 (pouring) cream
salt and black pepper
12 sheets of dried or fresh lasagne
50 g (1¾ oz/⅓ cup) grated Comté

40 × 20 cm (15¾ × 8 in) gratin dish

Preheat the oven to 180°C (350°F/Gas 4). Peel the sweet potatoes and cut them into thin rounds. Arrange them on a baking tray lined with greaseproof paper and drizzle with 3 tablespoons olive oil, followed by the honey. Sprinkle with the fleur de sel and some ground mixed peppercorns. Bake in the oven for 20 minutes.

Cut the pork into large cubes, then blitz in a food processor with the shallot, garlic, parsley and ½ tablespoon oregano. Season with salt and pepper. Heat a dash of olive oil in a frying pan (skillet) and gently fry the pork mixture for 5 minutes. Add the porcini mushrooms, stir and continue cooking for 5 minutes.

Mix the cream with the remaining 1 tablespoon oregano, and season with salt and pepper.

Pour 1 teaspoon olive oil and a little oregano cream into the bottom of the gratin dish. Lay 3 sheets of lasagne in the bottom of the dish, side by side, and then alternate layers of meat with mushrooms, lasagne, oregano cream and sweet potato. Sprinkle with cheese and bake in the oven for 30–40 minutes.

MEAT

MINCED LAMB
lasagne

Serves 6
Preparation: 45 minutes
Cooking time: 2 hours 45 minutes

2 tablespoons olive oil
  + 1 teaspoon olive oil
1 garlic clove, thinly sliced
1 large onion, thinly sliced
1 stick of celery, diced
300 g (10½ oz) carrots, diced
200 g (7 oz) smoked
  bacon slices, diced
200 g (7 oz) coarse pork
  sausage meat
500 g (1 lb 2 oz) minced
  (ground) lamb
200 ml (7 fl oz) red wine
80 ml (2½ fl oz) milk
300 ml passata (puréed tomatoes)
1 teaspoon sugar
salt and black pepper
2 aubergines (eggplants)
12 sheets of dried or fresh lasagne
80 g (2¾ oz/¾ cup grated
  Parmesan

40 × 20 cm (15¾ × 8 in) gratin dish

Heat 1 tablespoon olive oil in a frying pan (skillet) and fry the garlic, onion, celery, carrots and bacon over a low heat for 10 minutes. Turn the heat up to medium, then add the sausage meat, breaking it up with a wooden spoon, followed by the minced lamb. Stir well and fry for 5 minutes, stirring constantly, until the meat is browned. Pour in the red wine and simmer until it is reduced by half. Pour in the milk, then simmer for a further 10 minutes. Stir in the passata and sugar, and lightly season with salt and pepper. Simmer gently for 2 hours with the lid on.

Preheat the oven to 200°C (400°F/Gas 6). Wrap the whole aubergines in aluminium foil and put them in the oven for 20–25 minutes. Scoop out the flesh with a spoon and place in a bowl with 1 tablespoon olive oil. Season with salt and pepper.

Pour 1 teaspoon olive oil into the bottom of the gratin dish. Lay 3 sheets of lasagne in the bottom of the dish, side by side, then alternate layers of meat sauce, lasagne and aubergine. Repeat the process, finishing with a layer of meat sauce. Top with Parmesan and bake in the oven for 45 minutes. Keep an eye on the cooking – if the meat sauce seems dry, add a little water.

MEAT

LAMB AND PEA
lasagne

Serves 6
Preparation: 25 minutes
Cooking time: 30 minutes

2 teaspoons olive oil
2 sticks of celery, thinly sliced
1 garlic clove, thinly sliced
1 shallot, thinly sliced
600 g (1 lb 5 oz) shoulder
  of lamb or lamb mince
small bunch of mint, chopped
2 teaspoons ras el hanout
200 g (7 oz) fresh podded
  peas or frozen peas
300 ml (10 fl oz) chicken stock
600 ml (20½ fl oz) béchamel
  sauce (see page 4)
12 sheets of dried or fresh lasagne
80 g (2¾ oz/⅔ cup) grated Comté

40 × 20 cm (15¾ × 8 in) gratin dish

Preheat the oven to 200°C (400°F/Gas 6). Heat 1 teaspoon olive oil in a frying pan (skillet) and gently fry the celery, garlic and shallot for 5 minutes, until lightly browned.

If using lamb shoulder, finely chop the meat, or mince it in a food processor. Combine the minced lamb with the mint and 1 teaspoon ras el hanout in a bowl. Add the lamb to the pan, stir and allow it to brown for 5 minutes. Mix in the peas, then pour in enough chicken stock to reach halfway up the pan. Simmer over a low heat for 10 minutes.

Mix the béchamel sauce with the remaining 1 teaspoon ras el hanout.

Pour 1 teaspoon olive oil and a little of the spiced béchamel sauce into the bottom of the gratin dish. Lay 3 sheets of lasagne in the bottom of the dish, side by side, then alternate layers of lamb with peas, lasagne and béchamel sauce. Repeat the process, finishing with the béchamel sauce. Sprinkle over the grated cheese and bake in the oven for 25–30 minutes.

MEAT

RABBIT AND TOMATO
lasagne

Serves 6
Preparation: 30 minutes
Cooking time: 35 minutes

700 g (1 lb 9 oz) boneless
  rabbit (saddle or thighs)
1 tablespoon olive oil
1 garlic clove, thinly sliced
1 shallot, thinly sliced
50 ml (1¾ fl oz) chicken stock
500 ml (17 fl oz) tomato sauce
  (see page 4)
1 tablespoon tomato purée (paste)
salt and black pepper
1 tablespoon mustard
700 ml (23½ fl oz) béchamel
  sauce (see page 4)
12 sheets of dried or fresh lasagne
80 g (2¾ oz/⅔ cup) grated Comté
2 sprigs of fresh thyme
  or 2 teaspoons dried thyme

40 × 20 cm (15¾ × 8 in) gratin dish

Preheat the oven to 180°C (350°F/Gas 4). Cut the rabbit into small pieces. Heat the olive oil in a frying pan (skillet) and fry the garlic and shallot with the rabbit, until nicely browned. Pour in the chicken stock and stir well. Simmer for 15 minutes with the lid on. Pour in the tomato sauce and tomato purée, cover with the lid and cook, stirring, for a further 5 minutes. Season with salt and pepper.

Stir the mustard into the béchamel sauce.

Pour 1 ladleful of mustard béchamel sauce into the bottom of the gratin dish. Lay 3 sheets of lasagne in the bottom of the dish, side by side, and then alternate layers of rabbit sauce, lasagne and béchamel sauce. Repeat the process, finishing with béchamel sauce. Sprinkle with cheese and thyme, then bake in the oven for 35 minutes.

MEAT

HAM AND TOMATO
lasagne

Serves 6
Preparation: 15 minutes
Cooking time: 30 minutes

1 teaspoon olive oil
1 garlic clove, unpeeled
3 sprigs of thyme
500 ml (17 fl oz) tomato sauce
  (see page 4)
salt and black pepper
600 ml (20½ fl oz) béchamel
  sauce (see page 4)
12 sheets of dried or fresh lasagne
300 g (10½ oz) cooked ham
80 g (2¾ oz/¾ cup)
  grated Parmesan

40 × 20 cm (15¾ × 8 in) gratin dish

Preheat the oven to 180°C (350°F/Gas 4). Heat the olive oil in a frying pan (skillet), then fry the garlic clove and 2 sprigs of thyme until lightly coloured. Remove the garlic and thyme from the pan and discard. Pour the tomato sauce into the flavoured oil and allow to simmer gently for a few minutes. Season with salt and pepper.

Pour 1 ladleful of béchamel sauce into the gratin dish. Lay 3 sheets of lasagne in the bottom of the dish, side by side, then alternate layers of tomato sauce, lasagne, ham and béchamel sauce. Repeat the process, finishing with béchamel sauce. Sprinkle with Parmesan and thyme leaves. Season with pepper and bake in the oven for 30 minutes.

DELI

MUSHROOM PESTO
lasagne

Serves 6
Preparation: 25 minutes
Cooking time: 30–40 minutes

250 g (9 oz) goat's cheese
600 ml (20½ fl oz) warm
  béchamel sauce (see page 4)
1 teaspoon olive oil
12 sheets of dried or fresh lasagne
200 g (7 oz) rostello-
  style ham, sliced
50 g (1¾ oz/½ cup)
  grated Parmesan

MUSHROOM PESTO
400 g (14 oz) mushrooms
150 g (5½ oz/1 cup) hazelnuts
50 g (1¾ oz) Emmental
200 ml (7 fl oz) olive oil
zest and juice of 1 lemon
3 garlic cloves
5 sprigs of parsley
1 teaspoon flaked sea salt
freshly ground mixed peppercorns

40 × 20 cm (15¾ × 8 in) gratin dish

Preheat the oven to 180°C (350°F/Gas 4). For the mushroom pesto, blitz all of the ingredients together in a food processor.

Crumble the goat's cheese into the warm béchamel sauce and let it melt.

Pour 1 teaspoon olive oil and a little goat's cheese béchamel sauce into the bottom of the gratin dish. Lay 3 sheets of lasagne in the bottom of the dish, side by side, then alternate layers of mushroom pesto, ham, lasagne and béchamel sauce. Repeat the process, finishing with a layer of béchamel sauce. Top with Parmesan, then bake in the oven for 30–40 minutes.

DELI

CHEDDAR AND CHORIZO
lasagne

Serves 6
Preparation: 20 minutes
Cooking time: 30 minutes

1 teaspoon olive oil
1 onion, thinly sliced
1 garlic clove, thinly sliced
500 g (1 lb 2 oz) passata
1 tablespoon tomato purée (paste)
150 ml (5 fl oz) vegetable stock
3 sprigs of thyme
salt and black pepper
12 sheets of dried or fresh lasagne
200 g (7 oz) chorizo
  sausage, finely sliced
200 g (7 oz/1¾ cups)
  grated Cheddar

CREAMY BÉCHAMEL*
50 g (1¾ oz/¼ cup) butter
50 g (1¾ oz/½ cup) plain
  (all-purpose) flour
1 pinch of salt
300 ml (10 fl oz) vegetable stock
300 ml (10 fl oz) single
  (pouring) cream
30 g (1 oz/¼ cup) grated Cheddar
2 teaspoons paprika

40 × 20 cm (15¾ × 8 in) gratin dish

Preheat the oven to 180°C (350°F/Gas 4). Heat the olive oil in a frying pan (skillet) and fry the onion and garlic for 2 minutes. Pour in the passata and tomato purée, add a little vegetable stock and stir well. Add 2 thyme sprigs and season with salt and pepper.

For the béchamel sauce, melt the butter in a saucepan over a low heat. Add the flour and salt, then whisk continuously until it forms a paste. Pour in the remaining vegetable stock and cream, little by little, whisking constantly. The sauce should thicken and become smooth. Add the Cheddar and paprika, and season with salt.

Pour 1 ladleful of béchamel sauce into the bottom of a gratin dish. Lay 3 sheets of lasagne in the bottom of the dish, side by side, then alternate layers of tomato sauce, lasagne, tomato sauce, chorizo, béchamel sauce and lasagne. Repeat the process, finishing with a little béchamel sauce. Top with Cheddar, sprinkle with the remaining thyme and bake in the oven for 25–30 minutes.

*or 600 ml (20½ fl oz) classic béchamel sauce (see page 4)
  + 30 g (1 oz/¼ cup) grated Cheddar

DELI

LEEK AND CURED HAM
lasagne

Serves 6
Preparation: 20 minutes
Cooking time: 30 minutes

1 tablespoon olive oil
50 g (1¾ oz/¼ cup) butter
2 garlic cloves, thinly sliced
300 g (10½ oz) leeks, thinly sliced
200 ml (7 fl oz) vegetable stock
1 pinch of salt
1 pinch of freshly ground
  mixed peppercorns
600 ml (20½ fl oz) béchamel
  sauce (see page 4)
100 g (3½ oz/1 cup)
  grated Parmesan
12 sheets of dried or fresh lasagne
150 g (5½ oz) thinly
  sliced cured ham
100 g (3½ oz/⅔ cup) pine nuts
small bunch of chervil,
  finely chopped

40 × 20 cm (15¾ × 8 in) gratin dish

Preheat the oven to 180°C (350°F/Gas 4). Heat the olive oil and butter in a frying pan (skillet), add the garlic and leeks, and fry for a few minutes until the leeks are softened. Pour in the vegetable stock and bring to a simmer. Season with salt and ground mixed peppercorns. Continue to simmer for 5 minutes.

Stir together the béchamel sauce and Parmesan.

Pour 1 teaspoon olive oil and a little Parmesan béchamel sauce into the bottom of the gratin dish. Lay 3 sheets of lasagne in the bottom of the dish, side by side, then alternate layers of leeks, lasagne, béchamel sauce and cured ham. Repeat the process, finishing with béchamel sauce and a little ham. Sprinkle with pine nuts and chervil. Bake in the oven for 25–30 minutes.

DELI

MUSHROOM AND SPINACH
lasagne

Serves 6
Preparation: 25 minutes
Cooking time: 30 minutes

2 teaspoons olive oil
2 garlic cloves, chopped
1 shallot, chopped
100 g (3½ oz) coppa ham, chopped
500 g (1 lb 2 oz) mushrooms
   (variety of your choice), quartered
small bunch of parsley sprigs
400 g (14 oz) fresh spinach
   or 200 g (7 oz) frozen spinach
600 ml (20½ fl oz) béchamel
   sauce (see page 4)
salt and black pepper
12 sheets of dried or fresh lasagne
50 g (1¾ oz/½ cup) grated
   Parmesan
50 g (1¾ oz/⅓ cup) grated
   mozzarella
1 pinch of pink peppercorns

40 × 20 cm (15¾ × 8 in) gratin dish

Preheat the oven to 180°C (350°F/Gas 4). Heat 1 teaspoon olive oil in a frying pan (skillet), add the garlic, shallot, ham and mushrooms, and fry for a few minutes. Snip in the parsley, setting aside 4 sprigs for the béchamel sauce.

In a separate frying pan, cook the spinach in a little water for 5–10 minutes, until wilted. Remove from the heat, rinse in cold water, drain and squeeze dry with your hands.

Add the spinach to the béchamel sauce. Chop the remaining 4 sprigs of parsley, add to the béchamel sauce and season to taste.

Pour 1 teaspoon olive oil and a little spinach béchamel sauce into the bottom of the gratin dish. Lay 3 sheets of lasagne in the bottom of the dish, side by side, then alternate layers of mushrooms with coppa, lasagne and béchamel sauce. Repeat the process, finishing with a layer of béchamel sauce. Top with grated cheeses, sprinkle with pink peppercorns, then bake in the oven for 25–30 minutes.

DELI

SALMON AND PARMESAN
lasagne

Serves 6
Preparation: 40 minutes
Cooking time: 30 minutes

2 tablespoons fish stock powder
500 g (1 lb 2 oz) salmon fillets
1 teaspoon olive oil
½ garlic clove, thinly sliced
1 shallot, thinly sliced
500 g (1 lb 2 oz) fresh mussels
250 ml (8½ fl oz) white wine
1 pinch of ground coriander
12 sheets of dried or fresh lasagne
5 sprigs of dill, snipped
80 g (2¾ oz/¾ cup) grated
  Parmesan

MUSSEL BÉCHAMEL SAUCE*
2 tablespoons butter
4 tablespoons plain (all-purpose)
  flour
1 pinch of salt
200 ml (7 fl oz) mussel
  cooking juices
50 ml (1¾ fl oz) fish stock
2 tablespoons crème fraîche
1 pinch of ground nutmeg

*or 600 ml (20½ fl oz) classic
  béchamel sauce (see page 4)

40 × 20 cm (15¾ × 8 in) gratin dish

Preheat the oven to 180°C (350°F/Gas 4). Heat 500 ml (17 fl oz) water in a saucepan and add the fish stock powder. Poach the salmon fillets in the stock for 2–3 minutes, then drain. Use a fork to break up the salmon into large chunks and set aside.

Heat the olive oil in a frying pan (skillet), add the garlic and shallot and fry for 1 minute. Add the mussels, white wine and coriander. Cover and simmer for 5–8 minutes. As soon as the mussels open, take the pan off the heat and tip the contents into a sieve set over a bowl to catch the juices. Remove and discard the shells from the mussels and set aside.

For the béchamel sauce, melt the butter in a saucepan over a low heat. Add the flour and salt, then whisk continuously to form a paste. Pour in the mussel cooking juices, stirring constantly. Incorporate the fish stock, followed by the crème fraîche and nutmeg. The sauce should be nice and smooth.

Pour 1 ladleful of béchamel sauce into the bottom of the gratin dish. Lay 3 sheets of lasagne in the bottom of the dish, side by side, and then alternate layers of salmon, mussels, lasagne and béchamel sauce. Repeat the process, finishing with béchamel sauce. Sprinkle with dill and Parmesan. Bake in the oven for 30 minutes.

FISH

TROUT AND WATERCRESS
lasagne

Serves 6
Preparation: 15 minutes
Marinate: 30 minutes
Cooking time: 25 minutes

500 g (1 lb 2 oz) trout
   (or salmon) fillets
zest of 1 lime
1 pinch of ground pink peppercorns
2 tablespoons olive oil
   + 2 teaspoons olive oil
200 g (7 oz) watercress
1 garlic clove
1 shallot
salt and black pepper
600 ml (20½ fl oz) béchamel
   sauce (see page 4)
12 sheets of dried or fresh lasagne
100 g (3½ oz) mozzarella, sliced

40 × 20 cm (15¾ × 8 in) gratin dish

Cut the trout into strips and arrange on a dish, without overlapping. Sprinkle with lime zest and pink peppercorns, then drizzle with 2 tablespoons olive oil. Cover with cling film (plastic wrap), then chill for at least 30 minutes.

Preheat the oven to 180°C (350°F/Gas 4). Remove the thick stalks from the watercress, then put it in a food processor with the garlic and shallot and blitz to a rough paste. Heat 1 teaspoon olive oil in a frying pan (skillet) and fry the watercress paste briefly. Season with salt and pepper. Take off the heat and when cool, remove as much moisture as possible by squeezing the watercress with your hands.

Stir the cooked watercress into the béchamel sauce.

Drain the trout. Pour 1 teaspoon olive oil and a little béchamel sauce into the bottom of the gratin dish. Lay 3 sheets of lasagne in the bottom of the dish, side by side, then alternate layers of trout, lasagne and béchamel sauce. Repeat the process, finishing with a little béchamel sauce. Spread slices of mozzarella on top and bake in the oven for 25 minutes.

FISH

TUNA AND FETA
lasagne

Serves 6
Preparation: 20 minutes
Cooking time: 25 minutes

500 g (1 lb 2 oz) tinned tuna
  in brine
500 ml (17 fl oz) tomato sauce
  with olives or herbs (shop-bought
  or homemade, see page 4)
2 tablespoons caper berries
2 anchovy fillets in oil
1 garlic clove, chopped
300 g (10½ oz) feta
1 teaspoon olive oil
12 sheets of dried or fresh lasagne
200 ml (7 fl oz) fish stock
small bunch of parsley, chopped

40 × 20 cm (15¾ × 8 in) gratin dish

Preheat the oven to 180°C (350°F/Gas 4). Drain the tuna and put in a bowl with the tomato sauce. Mix together, breaking the tuna up with a fork. Add the caper berries, anchovy fillets and garlic.

Cut the feta into strips.

Pour the olive oil and a little tuna and tomato sauce into the bottom of the gratin dish. Lay 3 sheets of lasagne in the bottom of the dish, side by side, then alternate layers of feta, a ladleful of fish stock, lasagne, tuna and tomato sauce and chopped parsley. Repeat the process, finishing with some feta and a little parsley. Bake in the oven for 25 minutes.

FISH

SPINACH AND ANCHOVY
lasagne

Serves 6
Preparation: 35 minutes
Cooking time: 35 minutes

90 ml (3 fl oz) olive oil
1 knob of butter
1 garlic clove, thinly sliced
1 kg (2 lb 3 oz) fresh spinach
(or 450 g/1 lb frozen spinach)
flaked sea salt
freshly ground mixed peppercorns
250 g (9 oz/1 cup) ricotta
180 g (6½ oz/1¾ cups) grated
  Parmesan
5 anchovy fillets in oil
400 ml (13½ fl oz) tomato sauce
  (see page 4)
small bunch of basil, chopped
1 pinch of dried chilli flakes
12 sheets of dried or fresh lasagne
300 ml (10 fl oz) béchamel
  sauce (see page 4)
120 g (4½ oz) mozzarella, sliced

40 × 20 cm (15¾ × 8 in) gratin dish

Preheat the oven to 180°C (350°F/Gas 4). Heat 3 tablespoons olive oil and the butter in a frying pan (skillet), then add the garlic. Fry gently for 2 minutes, then add the spinach. Stir until the spinach wilts, then season with salt and pepper. Transfer to a bowl, allow to cool, then squeeze the spinach with your hands to remove as much water as possible. Chop the spinach roughly and put it in a bowl with the ricotta and 80 g (2¾ oz/¾ cup) grated Parmesan. Mix well.

Heat 2 tablespoons olive oil in a saucepan and add the anchovy fillets. Fry for 1 minute, crushing the anchovies lightly with a wooden spoon. Pour in the tomato sauce, then add the basil and chilli. Simmer for 10 minutes.

Pour 1 teaspoon olive oil and a little béchamel sauce into the bottom of the gratin dish. Lay 3 sheets of lasagne in the bottom of the dish, side by side, and then alternate layers of ricotta and spinach, lasagne and tomato sauce. Repeat the process, finishing with a layer of béchamel sauce. Top with slices of mozzarella and the remaining Parmesan. Bake in the oven for 35 minutes.

FISH

SEAFOOD
lasagne

Serves 6
Preparation: 25 minutes
Cooking time: 30 minutes

1 tablespoon olive oil
  + 1 teaspoon olive oil
½ fennel bulb, thinly sliced
1 stick of celery, thinly sliced
1 garlic clove, thinly sliced
1 shallot, thinly sliced
500 g (1 lb 2 oz) frozen mixed
  seafood
1 pinch of ground turmeric
½ teaspoon coriander seeds
300 g (10½ oz) white fish fillets,
  cut into small chunks
200 ml (7 fl oz) dry white wine
2 tablespoons crème fraîche
12 sheets of dried or fresh lasagne
500 ml (17 fl oz) shop-bought
  nantua sauce or béchamel sauce
  (see page 4)
80 g (2¾ oz/¾ cup) grated
  Parmesan

40 × 20 cm (15¾ × 8 in) gratin dish

Preheat the oven to 180°C (350°F/Gas 4). Heat 1 tablespoon olive oil in a frying pan (skillet) and fry the fennel, celery, garlic and shallots for a few minutes, until softened. Add the frozen seafood, stir, then add the turmeric, coriander seeds and white fish. Cook for 2 minutes, then pour in the white wine, cover with a lid and simmer for 10 minutes. Add the crème fraîche and stir gently.

Pour 1 teaspoon olive oil into the bottom of the gratin dish. Lay 3 sheets of lasagne in the bottom of the dish, side by side, then alternate layers of seafood, nantua sauce and lasagne. Repeat the process, finishing with a little sauce. Top with Parmesan and bake in the oven for 25–30 minutes.

FISH

CURRIED CRAB
lasagne

Serves 6
Preparation: 20 minutes
Cooking time: 25 minutes

2 tablespoons olive oil
½ fennel bulb, thinly sliced
½ garlic clove, crushed
small bunch of coriander
  (cilantro) or dill, chopped
3 pinches of flaked sea salt
500 g (1 lb 2 oz) crab meat
freshly ground mixed peppercorns
1 pinch of dried chilli flakes
1 teaspoon curry powder
½ teaspoon ground turmeric
700 ml (23½ fl oz) béchamel
  sauce (see page 4)
12 sheets of dried or fresh lasagne

40 × 20 cm (15¾ × 8 in) gratin dish

Preheat the oven to 180°C (350°F/Gas 4). Heat 1 tablespoon olive oil in a frying pan (skillet) and fry the fennel over a low heat, until softened. Add the garlic, 2 tablespoons chopped coriander or dill, and a pinch of salt. Cook gently for 5 minutes.

Set aside some of the coriander or dill to garnish. In a bowl, mix the crab meat with the remaining coriander or dill, 1 tablespoon olive oil, 2 pinches of salt and some pepper.

Stir the chilli, curry powder and turmeric into the béchamel sauce.

Pour a ladleful of béchamel sauce into the bottom of a gratin dish. Lay 3 sheets of lasagne in the bottom of the dish, side by side, then alternate layers of béchamel sauce, lasagne, crab and fennel. Repeat the process, finishing with a layer of béchamel sauce and garnish with coriander or dill. Bake in the oven for 25 minutes.

FISH

SPINACH AND RICOTTA
lasagne

Serves 6
Preparation: 30 minutes
Cooking time: 30–40 minutes

2 tablespoons olive oil
  + 1 teaspoon olive oil
1 knob of butter
2 garlic cloves, thinly sliced
½ teaspoon ground nutmeg
1 kg (2 lb 3 oz) fresh spinach
  (or 450 g/1 lb frozen spinach)
450 g (1 lb/1¾ cup) ricotta
200 g (7 oz/2 cups) grated
  Parmesan + 3 tablespoons
  for the béchamel sauce
salt and black pepper
600 ml (20½ fl oz) béchamel
  sauce (see page 4)
12 sheets of dried or fresh lasagne

40 × 20 cm (15¾ × 8 in) gratin dish

Preheat the oven to 180°C (350°F/Gas 4). Heat 2 tablespoons olive oil along with the butter in a frying pan (skillet). Add the garlic and nutmeg, fry for 2 minutes, then add the spinach. Cook until the spinach has wilted. Remove from the heat, allow to cool, then remove as much water as possible by squeezing the spinach with your hands. Roughly chop the spinach and put it in a bowl with the ricotta and 2 tablespoons grated Parmesan. Season with salt and pepper, and stir well.

Stir 3 tablespoons grated Parmesan into the béchamel sauce.

Pour 1 teaspoon olive oil into the bottom of the gratin dish. Lay 3 sheets of lasagne in the bottom of the dish, side by side, then alternate layers of spinach and ricotta mixture, lasagne and béchamel sauce. Repeat the process, finishing with a layer of béchamel sauce. Top with the remaining Parmesan and bake in the oven for 30–40 minutes.

VEGETABLES

TOMATO AND MOZZARELLA
lasagne

Serves 6
Preparation: 25 minutes
Cooking time: 30–40 minutes

1 tablespoon olive oil
  + 1 teaspoon olive oil
1 knob of butter
1 garlic clove, thinly sliced
2 spring onions (scallions)
2 sprigs of oregano
  (or 1 teaspoon dried oregano)
800 g (1 lb 12 oz) peeled
  and chopped tomatoes
1 pinch of sugar
salt and black pepper
very small bunch of basil
500 g (1 lb 2 oz) mozzarella
12 sheets of dried or fresh lasagne
80 g (2¾ oz/¾ cup)
  grated Parmesan

40 × 20 cm (15¾ × 8 in) gratin dish

Preheat the oven to 150°C (300°F/Gas 2). Heat 1 tablespoon olive oil and the butter in a frying pan (skillet), then add the garlic, spring onions and oregano. Fry for 2 minutes, then add the tomatoes, sugar and 1 pinch each of salt and pepper. Simmer over a medium heat for 20 minutes, with the lid on. Add a handful of snipped basil leaves and continue cooking for 5 minutes.

Cut the mozzarella into slices about 0.5 cm (¼ in) thick.

Pour 1 teaspoon olive oil into the bottom of the gratin dish. Lay 3 sheets of lasagne in the bottom of the dish, side by side, then alternate layers of tomato sauce, lasagne, mozzarella, a few basil leaves and a dash of olive oil. Repeat the process, finishing with slices of mozzarella. Sprinkle with Parmesan and bake in the oven for 30–40 minutes.

VEGETABLES

VEGETARIAN
lasagne

Serves 6
Preparation: 30 minutes
Cooking time: 30 minutes

3 tablespoons olive oil
1 garlic clove, thinly sliced
1 onion, thinly sliced
1 aubergine (eggplant), diced
2 courgettes (zucchini), diced
4 sprigs of thyme (or 3 teaspoons
    of dried thyme)
100 g (3½ oz) young spinach leaves
500 ml (17 fl oz) tomato
    sauce (see page 4)
salt and pepper
12 sheets of dried or fresh lasagne
300 g (10½ oz) jarred roasted
    peppers, cut into strips
600 ml (20½ fl oz) béchamel sauce
    (see page 4)
80 g (2¾ oz/¾ cup) grated
    Parmesan

40 × 20 cm (15¾ × 8 in) gratin dish

Preheat the oven to 180°C (350°F/Gas 4). Heat the olive oil in a frying pan (skillet) and fry the garlic, onion, aubergine and courgettes for a few minutes. Add the leaves from 3 sprigs of thyme, or 2 teaspoons dried thyme, and the spinach leaves, then stir. Cook gently for 10 minutes over a low heat, then add the tomato sauce. Season.

Pour 1 ladleful of béchamel sauce into the bottom of the gratin dish. Lay 3 sheets of lasagne in the bottom of the dish, side by side, then alternate layers of stewed vegetables, peppers cut into strips and béchamel sauce. Repeat the process, finishing with béchamel sauce. Sprinkle with Parmesan and the remaining thyme. Bake in the oven for 30 minutes.

VEGETABLES

AUBERGINE AND PESTO
lasagne

Serves 6
Preparation: 30 minutes
Cooking time: 50 minutes

1 aubergine (eggplant)
salt and black pepper
100 ml (3½ fl oz) olive oil
  + 1 teaspoon olive oil
2 tomatoes, sliced
3 tablespoons shop-bought
  basil pesto (or see page 68)
600 g (1 lb 5 oz) fresh spinach
  or 300 g (10½ oz) frozen spinach
600 ml (20½ fl oz) béchamel
  sauce (see page 4)
2 tablespoons ricotta
120 g (4½ oz/1¼ cups) grated
  Parmesan
12 sheets of dried or fresh lasagne
200 g (7 oz/1⅓ cups) grated
  mozzarella
small bunch of basil leaves, snipped

40 × 20 cm (15¾ × 8 in) gratin dish

Cut the aubergine into rounds 0.5 cm (¼ in) thick and sprinkle with salt and pepper on both sides. Heat 100 ml (3½ fl oz) olive oil in a frying pan (skillet) until it shimmers, without smoking. Fry the aubergines on both sides for a few minutes, until golden. Remove and drain on kitchen paper. Alternatively, bake in the oven: preheat the oven to 200°C (400°F/Gas 6), then arrange the aubergine rounds on a baking tray lined with greaseproof paper, drizzle with olive oil and season. Roast for 15–20 minutes.

Preheat the oven to 160°C (325°F/Gas 3). Brush the tomato slices on both sides with 1 tablespoon pesto.

Wilt the spinach in a frying pan with a little water for 5–10 minutes, stirring.

Mix the béchamel sauce with the remaining 2 tablespoons pesto, the ricotta, 3 tablespoons grated Parmesan and a few snipped basil leaves. Adjust the seasoning if necessary.

Pour 1 teaspoon olive oil into the bottom of the gratin dish. Lay 3 sheets of lasagne in the bottom of the dish, side by side, then add alternate layers of spinach, lasagne, béchamel sauce with pesto, lasagne, roast aubergine, lasagne, tomatoes with pesto. Finish with a little béchamel sauce. Top with mozzarella, the remaining Parmesan and the basil leaves. Bake in the oven for 25–30 minutes.

VEGETABLES

ARTICHOKE
lasagne

Serves 6
Preparation: 15 minutes
Cooking time: 25 minutes

500 g (1 lb 2 oz) artichokes in oil
150 g (5½ oz) radicchio, thinly
   sliced
1 handful of rocket (arugula),
   snipped
500 g (1 lb 2 oz/2 cups) ricotta
½ garlic clove, chopped
a few sage leaves, chopped
salt and black pepper
2 teaspoons olive oil
12 sheets of dried or fresh lasagne
8 sun-dried tomatoes
3 tablespoons grated Parmesan

40 × 20 cm (15¾ × 8 in) gratin dish

Preheat the oven to 160°C (325°F/Gas 3). Drain the artichokes and cut them into thin strips.

In a bowl, combine the radicchio, rocket, ricotta, garlic and sage. Add 1 pinch each of salt and pepper.

Pour the olive oil into the bottom of the gratin dish. Lay 3 sheets of lasagne in the bottom of the dish, side by side, then alternate layers of ricotta with rocket and radicchio, lasagne and artichokes. Repeat the process, finishing with ricotta. Top with the sun-dried tomatoes and sprinkle with Parmesan. Bake in the oven for 25 minutes.

VEGETABLES

POTATO
lasagne

Serves 6
Preparation: 25 minutes
Cooking time: 45 minutes

400 g (14 oz) courgettes (zucchini)
400 g (14 oz) potatoes, peeled
300 ml (10 fl oz) crème fraîche
200 g (7 oz/scant 2 cups)
  mascarpone
salt and black pepper
small handful of basil leaves
12 sheets of dried or fresh lasagne
150 g (5½ oz) smoked cheese,
  such as scamorza, cut into strips
150 g (5½ oz/1 cup) grated Comté

40 × 20 cm (15¾ × 8 in) gratin dish

Preheat the oven to 200°C (400°F/Gas 6). Cut the courgettes and potatoes into fine discs, preferably with a mandoline or a food processor fitted with the slicing disc.

In a bowl, mix the crème fraîche, mascarpone, 1 pinch each of salt and pepper and a few snipped basil leaves.

Pour 1 layer of crème fraîche onto the bottom of the gratin dish. Lay 3 sheets of lasagne in the bottom of the dish, side by side, then alternate layers of potatoes, crème fraîche, potatoes, strips of smoked cheese and courgettes. Repeat the process, seasoning between each layer. Finish with a layer of crème fraîche. Top with Comté, sprinkle with a few basil leaves and bake in the oven for 30 minutes. Reduce the oven temperature to 180°C (350°F/Gas 4) and bake for a further 15 minutes.

VEGETABLES

GREEN VEGETABLE
lasagne

Serves 6
Preparation: 25 minutes
Cooking time: 25 minutes

2 tablespoons olive oil
  + 1 teaspoon olive oil
3 garlic cloves, chopped
3 small spring onions (scallions),
  thinly sliced
500 g (1 lb 2 oz) asparagus spears
400 g (14 oz) shelled peas
250 g (9 oz) shelled broad beans
salt and black pepper
200 ml (7 fl oz) hot vegetable
  stock
small bunch of mint, snipped
300 ml (10 fl oz) single (pouring)
  cream
250 g (9 oz/1 cup) cottage cheese
250 g (9 oz/1 cup) cream cheese
zest of ½ lemon
12 sheets of dried or fresh lasagne
100 g (3½ oz/1 cup) grated
  Parmesan

40 × 20 cm (15¾ × 8 in) gratin dish

Preheat the oven to 160°C (325°F/Gas 3). Heat 2 tablespoons olive oil in a frying pan (skillet) and fry the garlic and spring onions.

Peel the asparagus spears and cut them into small 2 cm (¾ in) sections, and set the tips aside. Add the asparagus, peas and broad beans to the pan, season with salt and pepper, then pour in the hot stock. Simmer gently for 5–8 minutes.

In a bowl, mix the mint with the cream, cottage cheese and cream cheese. Add the lemon zest and season.

Pour 1 teaspoon olive oil into the bottom of the gratin dish. Lay 3 sheets of lasagne in the bottom of the dish, side by side, then alternate layers of green vegetables, lasagne, Parmesan and minted cream. Repeat the process, finishing with the reserved asparagus tips and a layer of cream. Sprinkle with grated Parmesan and bake in the oven for 20–25 minutes or put under the grill for 15 minutes.

VEGETABLES

GREENS AND GOAT'S CHEESE
lasagne

Serves 6
Preparation: 20 minutes
Cooking time: 25 minutes

1 kg (2 lb 3 oz) Swiss chard
500 g (1 lb 2 oz) fresh spinach
  or 250 g (9 oz) frozen spinach
2 teaspoons olive oil
2 garlic cloves, thinly sliced
salt and black pepper
1 ash-coated goat's cheese
400 g (14 oz) fresh goat's cheese
300 ml (10 fl oz) single
  (pouring) cream
2 sprigs of thyme (or
  2 teaspoons dried thyme)
12 sheets of dried or fresh lasagne
150 ml (5 fl oz) milk

40 × 20 cm (15¾ × 8 in) gratin dish

Preheat the oven to 180°C (350°F/Gas 4). Rinse the Swiss chard and spinach. Trim off the stalks from the Swiss chard and roughly chop the leaves with the spinach.

Heat 1 teaspoon olive oil in a frying pan (skillet), add the garlic and fry for 2 minutes. Add the Swiss chard and spinach, fry briefly, then cover with a lid and let the vegetables wilt for a few minutes. Remove the lid and continue to cook over a medium heat to allow the water to evaporate. Season with salt and pepper.

Set aside a few thin slices of the ash-coated goat's cheese for the garnish. Gently melt the remaining ash-coated goat's cheese and the fresh goat's cheese with the cream and thyme in a saucepan. Season with salt and pepper.

Pour 1 teaspoon olive oil and a little goat's cheese cream into the bottom of the gratin dish. Lay 3 sheets of lasagne in the bottom of the dish, side by side, and then alternate layers of spinach and Swiss chard, sheets of lasagne and goat's cheese cream. Repeat the process, finishing with a layer of cream. Top with the reserved slices of ash-coated goat's cheese, pour the milk on top and bake in the oven for 25 minutes.

VEGETABLES

ASPARAGUS AND EGG
lasagne

Serves 6
Preparation: 15 minutes
Cooking time: 30 minutes

6 hard-boiled eggs
500 g (1 lb 2 oz) jarred cooked
  white asparagus spears
2 tablespoons butter
4 tablespoons flour
1 pinch of salt
250 ml (8½ fl oz) milk
250 ml (8½ fl oz) single (pouring)
  cream
1 pinch of ground nutmeg
small bunch of chives, snipped
12 sheets of dried or fresh lasagne
100 g (3½ oz/1 cup) grated
  Parmesan

40 × 20 cm (15¾ × 8 in) gratin dish

Preheat the oven to 180°C (350°F/Gas 4). Peel the eggs, then cut them into rounds, not too thin. Drain the asparagus and pat dry with kitchen paper.

Melt the butter in a saucepan over a low heat. Add the flour and salt, then whisk constantly to form a paste. Pour in the milk and cream, little by little, stirring continuously. The sauce should thicken and become a smooth béchamel sauce. Add the nutmeg and most of the chives, reserving 2 pinches for the topping.

Pour 1 ladleful of the chive béchamel sauce into the bottom of the gratin dish. Lay 3 sheets of lasagne in the bottom of the dish, side by side, then alternate layers of sliced egg, béchamel sauce, lasagne and asparagus. Repeat the process, finishing with chive béchamel sauce. Sprinkle with Parmesan and the reserved chives. Bake in the oven for 30 minutes.

VEGETABLES

BUTTERNUT AND TOMME
lasagne

Serves 6
Preparation: 30 minutes
Cooking time: 55 minutes

1 kg (2 lb 3 oz) butternut
  squash (pumpkin)
50 ml (1¾ fl oz) olive oil
1 garlic clove, thinly sliced
2 sprigs of rosemary, leaves picked
280 g (10 oz) sheep's milk tomme
a few sage leaves, snipped
600 ml (20½ fl oz) béchamel
  sauce (see page 4)
12 sheets of dried or fresh lasagne

40 × 20 cm (15¾ × 8 in) gratin dish

Preheat the oven to 200°C (400°F/Gas 6). Peel and deseed the squash, and cut the flesh into 0.5 cm (¼ in) thick slices. Lay the slices on a baking tray lined with greaseproof paper and drizzle with olive oil. Sprinkle with the garlic and most of the rosemary leaves. Roast in the oven for 25 minutes, until tender and golden brown.

Grate 80 g (2¾ oz) tomme into the béchamel sauce and stir in the sage.

Reduce the oven temperature to 180°C (350°F/Gas 4). Cut the remaining 200 g (7 oz) tomme into slices. Pour 1 ladleful of béchamel sauce into the bottom of the gratin dish. Lay 3 sheets of lasagne in the bottom of the dish, side by side, then alternate layers of butternut squash, béchamel sauce, tomme and lasagne. Repeat the process finishing with béchamel sauce and tomme. Sprinkle with the reserved rosemary and bake in the oven for 30 minutes.

VEGETABLES

COURGETTE AND PESTO
lasagne

Serves 6
Marinate: 1 hour
Preparation: 20 minutes
Rest: 1 hour

1 yellow courgette (zucchini)
1 green courgette (zucchini)
30 g (1 oz) salt
250 g (9 oz) feta or cottage cheese
50 ml (1¾ fl oz) milk
400 g (14 oz) chopped tomatoes
2 tablespoons olive oil
small bunch of chives, chopped
small bunch of parsley, chopped
flaked sea salt
freshly ground mixed peppercorns

BASIL PESTO
small bunch of basil
1 garlic clove
zest and juice of 1 lemon
50 g (1¾ oz/⅓ cup)
  macadamia nuts
70 ml (2¼ fl oz) olive oil

40 × 20 cm (15¾ × 8 in) gratin dish

Slice the courgettes lengthways into thin ribbons, using a mandoline or vegetable peeler. Arrange the courgette ribbons in a shallow dish, sprinkle with salt on both sides and leave to soften for 1 hour. Rinse them in cold water and drain on kitchen paper.

In a bowl, mix the cheese with the milk using a fork. In another bowl, mix the chopped tomatoes with 2 tablespoons olive oil, the snipped chives (setting a little aside for the garnish) and parsley. Season with salt and pepper.

For the pesto, blitz the basil, garlic, lemon zest and juice and macadamia nuts in a food processor. Gradually pour in the olive oil a little at a time to make a smooth pesto.

In a gratin dish, alternate layers of raw courgettes, pesto, tomato sauce and fresh cheese. Repeat the process, finishing with courgettes and sprinkling with the reserved snipped chives. Chill for at least 1 hour.

VEGETABLES

FOUR CHEESE
lasagne

Serves 6
Preparation: 20 minutes
Cooking time: 25 minutes

200 ml (7 fl oz) single
  (pouring) cream
150 g (5½ oz) gorgonzola
250 g (9 oz/1 cup) cottage cheese
  (or other fresh cheese)
1 teaspoon olive oil
12 sheets of dried or fresh lasagne
150 g (5½ oz) goat's cheese, sliced
150 g (5½ oz) mozzarella, sliced

40 × 20 cm (15¾ × 8 in) gratin dish

Preheat the oven to 180°C (350°F/Gas 4). Heat the cream in a saucepan, crumble in the gorgonzola and add the cottage cheese. Stir and allow the cheeses to gently melt into the cream for 5 minutes.

Pour the olive oil and a little cream and cheese mixture into the bottom of the gratin dish. Lay 3 sheets of lasagne, side by side, and then alternate layers of cream and cheese mixture, sheets of lasagne, goat's cheese, lasagne and mozzarella. Repeat the process, finishing with the cream and cheese mixture and bake in the oven for 25 minutes. Allow to rest for 5 minutes before serving as the hot lasagne will be very liquid.

CHEESE

ACKNOWLEDGEMENTS

My thanks to my assistant Eléa di Lorenzo, who cooks and helps me write these recipes with great professionalism and patience.

Thanks also to Anne, Rose-Marie and Emmanuel.

Thanks to Pauline. It is always a pleasure to work with you as we understand one another so well.

Thanks to Aurélie for her help in proofreading and her practised eye.

Thanks to my personal 'taster', who is now a specialist in lasagne.

Thanks to Sky MacAlpine for her recipe for hard-boiled egg lasagne.

And thanks to my little Lou for all the energy I get from you.

Lasagne by Sandra Mahut

First published in 2016 by Hachette Books (Marabout)

This English hardback edition published in 2017 by Hardie Grant Books

Hardie Grant Books (UK)
52-54 Southwark Street
London SE1 1UN
hardiegrant.co.uk

Hardie Grant Books (Australia)
Ground Floor, Building 1
658 Church Street
Melbourne, VIC 3121
hardiegrant.com.au

British Library Cataloguing-in-Publication Data. A catalogue record for this book is available from the British Library.

ISBN: 978-1-78488-125-2

Design: Frédéric Voisin
Illustration: Minsk Studio
Editing: Aurélie Legay, Véronique Dussidour, Natacha Kotchetkova

For the English hardback edition:
Publisher: Kate Pollard
Senior Editor: Kajal Mistry
Editorial Assistant: Hannah Roberts
Publishing Assistant: Eila Purvis
Translation: Gilla Evans
Copy editing: Kate Wanwimolruk
Typesetter: David Meikle
Colour Reproduction by p2d

Printed and bound in China by 1010

10 9 8 7 6 5 4 3 2 1